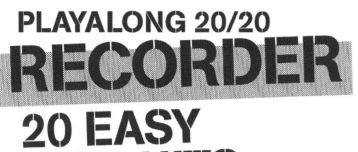

PLAYALONG 20/20
RECORDER
20 EASY POP HITS

T0078998

To acces audio visit:
www.halleonard.com/mylibrary
Enter Code:

5570-0175-8332-4011

Recorder Fingering Chart

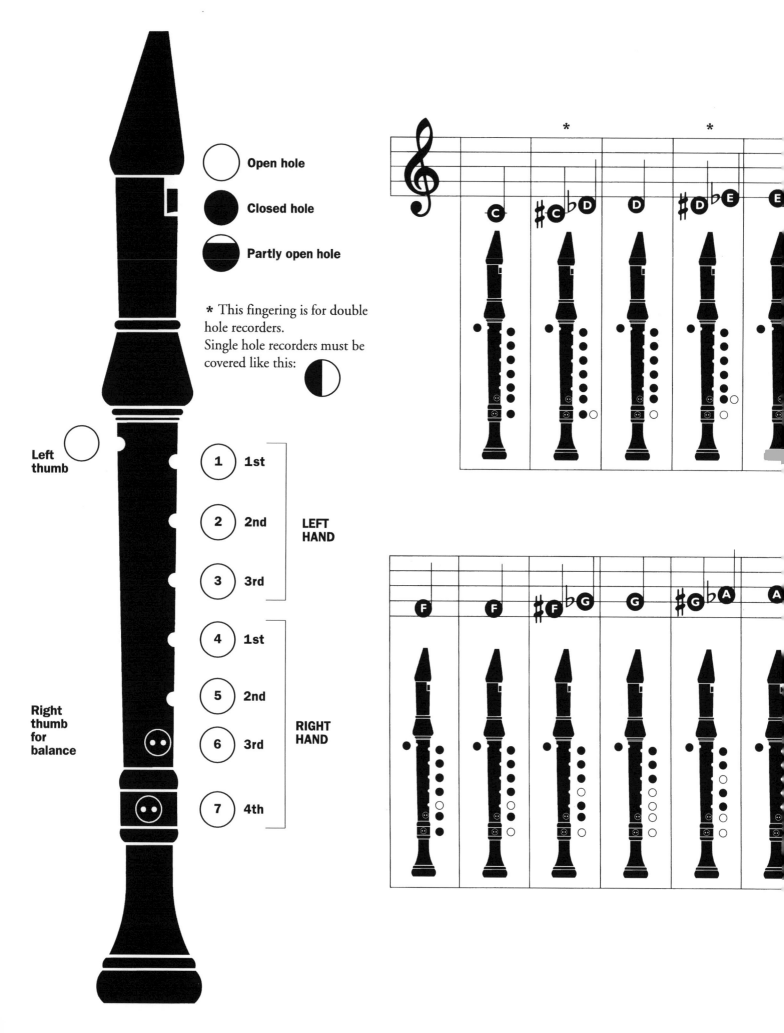

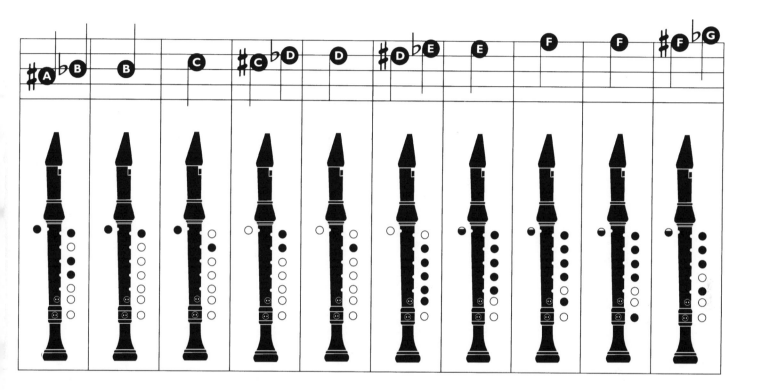

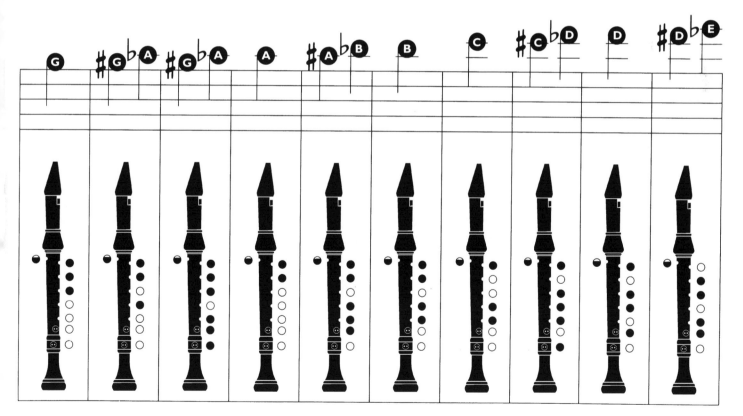

Arrangements by Christopher Hussey.
Backing tracks by Jeremy Birchall & Christopher Hussey.
Recorder played by Louise Bradbury.
Audio recorded, mixed and mastered by
Jonas Persson & Imogen Hall.

Order No.AM1010691
Printed in the EU.

ISBN: 978-1-78305-985-0

Visit Hal Leonard Online at
www.halleonard.com

Contact us:
Hal Leonard
7777 West Bluemound Road
Milwaukee, WI 53213
Email: info@halleonard.com

In Europe, contact:
Hal Leonard Europe Limited
42 Wigmore Street
Marylebone, London, W1U 2RY
Email: info@halleonardeurope.com

In Australia, contact:
Hal Leonard Australia Pty. Ltd.
4 Lentara Court
Cheltenham, Victoria, 3192 Australia
Email: info@halleonard.com.au

Let It Go (from *Frozen*)

Words & Music by Kirsten Anderson-Lopez and Robert Lopez

Expressively ♩ = 68

7

22 (Taylor Swift)

Words & Music by Taylor Swift, Max Martin & Johan Schuster

Lightly and excitedly ♩ = 104

to Coda ⊕

D.S. al Coda

mp　　　　　　　　　　　　　　　*f*

⊕ **Coda**

All Of Me (John Legend)

Words & Music by John Stephens and Toby Gad

Passionately ♩ = 126

(piano cue)

to Coda ⊕

D.S. al Coda ⊕ **Coda**

Atlas (from *The Hunger Games: Catching Fire*)

Words & Music by Guy Berryman, Jonathan Buckland, William Champion & Christopher Martin

Melancholically ♩ = 137

(piano cue)

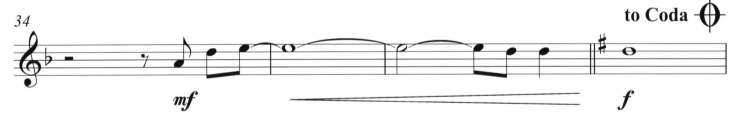

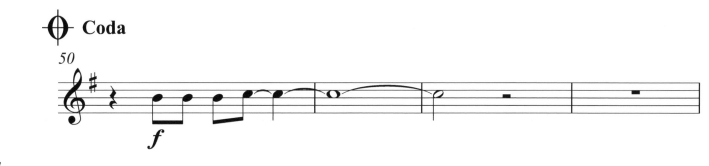

Coda

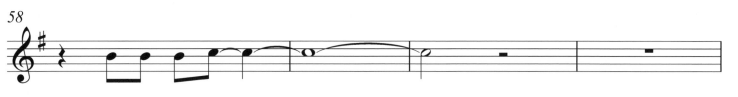

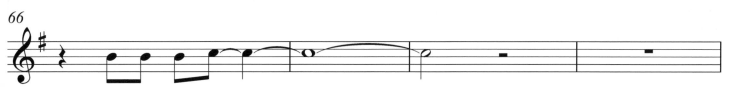

Best Song Ever (One Direction)

Words & Music by Wayne Hector, John Ryan, Julian Bunetta & Edward Drewett

Energetically ♩ = 118

Jar Of Hearts (Christina Perri)

Words & Music by Christina Perri, Drew Lawrence & Barrett Yeretsian

Passionately ♩ = 75

(piano cue)   *mp*

mf

mp   *mf*

to Coda ⊕

f

1.

mf

f

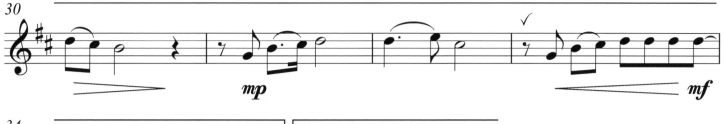

D.S. al Coda   **Coda**

molto rit.

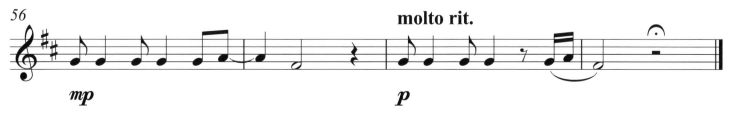

Just Give Me A Reason (Pink)

Words & Music by Alecia Moore, Jeff Bhasker & Nate Ruess

Passionately ♩ = 95

mf espressivo

Last Friday Night (Katy Perry)

Words & Music by Max Martin, Lukasz Gottwald, Bonnie McKee & Katy Perry

to Coda ⊕

1.

mf

2. (sax solo) **D.S. al Coda**

f

⊕ **Coda**

mf

Make You Feel My Love (Adele)

Words & Music by Bob Dylan

Tenderly ♩ = 76

mf dolce

f espressivo

mp

mf   mp

mf dolce

8

f espressivo

_mf_

_f_   _mp_

mp dolce

rit.

_p_

Once Upon A Dream (from *Maleficent*)

Words & Music by Sammy Fain & Jack Lawrence

Lazily ♩ = 120

(strings cue)

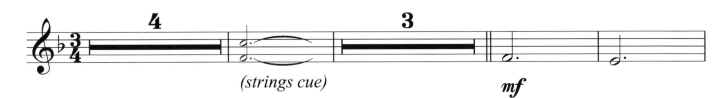

poco cresc.

Panic Cord (Gabrielle Aplin)

Words & Music by Jez Ashurst, Gabrielle Aplin & Nicholas Atkinson

Steadily, with a bounce ♩ = 106

(synth. vocals cue)

mf

mp

f

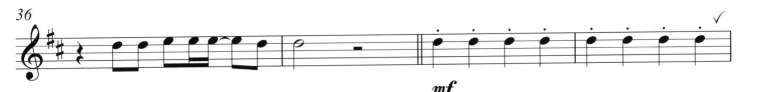

Right Place Right Time (Olly Murs)

Words & Music by Stephen Robson, Claude Kelly & Oliver Murs

Smoothly, with expression ♩ = 140

f legato

D.S. al Coda

Coda

mf

f

mf

Say Something (A Great Big World, feat. Christina Aguilera)

Words & Music by Mike Campbell, Chad Vaccarino & Ian Axel

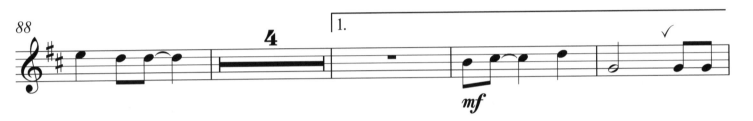

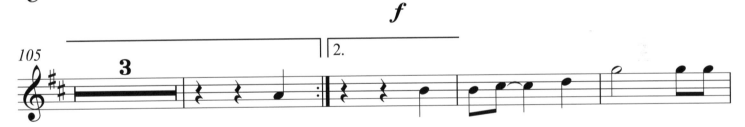

A Sky Full Of Stars (Coldplay)

Words & Music by Guy Berryman, Jonathan Buckland, William Champion, Christopher Martin & Tim Bergling

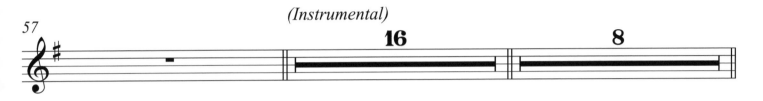

Stay (Rihanna, feat. Mikky Ekko)

Words & Music by Justin Parker & Mikky Ekko

Tenderly ♩ = 112

Titanium (David Guetta)

Words & Music by Sia Furler, David Guetta, Giorgio Tuinfort & Nick van de Wall

Energetically ♩ = 126

What Makes You Beautiful (One Direction)

Words & Music by Savan Kotecha, Carl Falk & Rami Yacoub

Steadily and smoothly ♩ = 125

to Coda ⊕

D.S. al Coda

⊕ **Coda**

Wrecking Ball (Miley Cyrus)

Words & Music by Stephan Moccio, Sacha Skarbek, Lukasz Gottwald, Henry Russell Walter & Maureen McDonald

to Coda

mf

mp

D.S. al Coda

f

Coda

mf

Someone Like You (Adele)

Words & Music by Daniel Wilson & Adele Adkins

poco rit.

A tempo

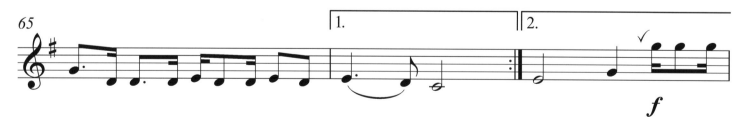

Skyfall (from *Skyfall*)

Words & Music by Adele Adkins & Paul Epworth

Powerfully ♩ = 75

(piano)   *mp*

(brass cue)

molto rit.

Freely